American Government in Action

The Congress of the United States

Michael Kronenwetter

Enslow Publishers, Inc.

44 Fadem Road   PO Box 38
Box 699   Aldershot
Springfield, NJ 07081 Hants GU12 6BP
USA   UK

Library of Congress Cataloging-in-Publication Data

Kronenwetter, Michael.
      The Congress of the United States / Michael Kronenwetter.
         p. cm. — (American government in action)
      Includes bibliographical references and index.
      Summary: Discusses the history, purpose, and functioning of the
Congress of the United States and the issues facing the legislative
branch of government at the end of the twentieth century.
      ISBN 0-89490-745-X
      1. United States. Congress—Juvenile literature. 2. United
States—Politics and government—Juvenile literature. [1. United
States. Congress. 2. United States—Politics and government.] I.
Title. II. Series.
JK1025.K76 1996
328.73'07'09—dc20   96-3848
                                    CIP
                                      AC

Printed in the United States of America

10 9 8 7 6 5 4 3 2 1

Illustration Credits:
Courtesy of Bob Dole, p. 86; courtesy of Byron Dorgan, p. 58;
courtesy of Newt Gingrich, p. 60; courtesy of Richard Gephardt,
p. 84; Library of Congress, pp. 23, 37, 54; photo by Michael
Kronenwetter, pp. 4, 19, 48, 81; The White House, pp. 74, 92;
United States Capitol, p. 42.

Cover Illustration: United States Capitol

Contents

The United States Capitol as it appears today

Bringing Down a President

On May 17, 1973, a number of men gathered behind a long table in the Senate Caucus Room. Photographers sat or squatted on the floor in front of them, snapping their pictures. From farther away, television cameras focused in, while television and microphone cables snaked through the aisles. Reporters, lawyers, and other spectators filled the seats reserved for the audience.

Who were these men, and what were they doing there? Why was everyone—including millions of Americans watching on television—waiting to see what they would do?

The men were, in fact, United States senators. They were members of a special Senate committee known across the country as the Watergate

Committee. And they were there to sit in judgment on the actions of the President of the United States.

Specifically they were investigating charges of criminal activity by the 1972 re-election campaign of President Richard Nixon. Nixon, a Republican, had been re-elected by a landslide, and yet a cloud hung over the White House. During the campaign, burglars had been caught breaking into the headquarters of the rival campaigners at the Watergate Hotel in Washington, D.C. Some of the burglars had been employees of President Nixon's campaign.

In effect the criminals had been working for the President. But, did the President know what they were doing? Had he ordered the break-in? Was the President of the United States a criminal?

"What did the President know?" asked Senator Howard Baker of Tennessee. "And when did he know it?" These, said Baker, were the questions the committee had to answer on behalf of the American people. Using its powers to investigate almost any matter involving the federal government, the Senate had appointed the Watergate Committee to find out the truth.

Week after week members of the President's staff paraded into the Senate Caucus Room. One after another they were grilled by the senators. Finally the truth came out—the President *had* been involved in criminal activity!

It was never actually proved that the President had ordered the burglary. He may not have even known it was going to happen. But the burglary was only part of the campaign's illegal activities. White House officials had been involved in all kinds of bad behavior, involving secret money and efforts to use the power of the government to frighten and punish political opponents of the President. And the President had known about a lot of these activities.

And all the while live television cameras broadcast the hearings. It was an amazing spectacle: one branch of the United States government exposing the corruption of another branch on live television.

But what would happen next? What *could* happen? What can be done when the President of the United States is guilty of a crime? Who, or what, is powerful enough to challenge the most powerful individual in the United States, and perhaps, in the world? The answer is the Congress of the United States—the Senate and the House of Representatives.

▶ Impeachment

The Senate committee had done its part. Now the House of Representatives had its own job to do. Under the United States Constitution, the House has the power to impeach—or charge—a President with "high crimes and misdemeanors."[1] When it does so, the charge is sent to the Senate for a trial. If the Senate finds the President guilty, he or she must leave office.

The question of whether to impeach President Nixon went first to the House Judiciary Committee. That committee would recommend to the whole House what it should do. By the time the committee met to vote, it was clear to everyone—except Nixon's most diehard supporters—that the President had misbehaved in office.

In one of the most solemn moments in the history of Congress, the House Judiciary Committee voted, 27 to 11, to recommend the impeachment of the President of the United States.

The impeachment procedure had only been used once before. Not long after the Civil War (1861–1865), the House impeached President Andrew Johnson. He was acquitted by one vote in the Senate trial. With all the evidence against President Nixon, and with the Senate in the hands of the Democrats, an acquittal was not likely this time.

President Nixon realized that his trial would divide the nation and that he was almost certain to be convicted and thrown out of office. Seeing no other choice, he resigned the presidency. His Vice President, Gerald Ford, became President. For the first time in history, Congress had, in effect, removed a President from office.

President Ford soon pardoned Richard Nixon for whatever crimes he had committed. Some people felt that Nixon had been treated unfairly. Others felt that he deserved exactly what he got. Still others felt that he escaped too easily. Many of his aides had gone to jail for their part in the Watergate affair. Why not the President, who had been their boss?

Most members of Congress, however, were pleased with the way they had handled the Watergate affair. Both houses of Congress had acted, and the President was out of office. This was, most of them believed, the best possible outcome for the nation. Now the political divisions might begin to heal, and Congress could get back to its main job of passing the nation's laws.

Whatever anyone thought about the outcome of the Watergate affair, it was an awesome display of the power of the United States Congress.

In this book we will explore this powerful and complicated institution—the first branch of the United States government.

The Birth of Congress

The body politic is sometimes compared to a living creature. Like a human being it has a soul or spirit, arms and legs, a conscience, and a brain.

In the United States the soul of this creature is the American people. In theory, at least, the government exists to serve the people and to do their will.

The executive branch—made up of the President and the federal departments under the President's control—is the arms and legs of the body politic. It performs the day-to-day chores of government: guarding the borders, maintaining the military, collecting taxes, enforcing federal regulations, and generally keeping the machinery of the government in working order.

The federal courts, led by the United States

Supreme Court, are the conscience of the government. They enforce the laws that keep the government honest and prevent it from violating the people's rights.

But the *brain* of the body politic—the organ that decides what the United States government is going to do—is the Congress. It is Congress that takes the will of the people and translates it into the plans and programs that the executive branch carries out and that the courts enforce.

More than either the President or the courts, Congress embodies the fundamental principle of American government—representative democracy.

▶ What Is a Representative?

The revolutionaries who drove the British out of the American colonies more than two hundred years ago resented the fact that the government of Britain levied taxes on the colonies without giving the colonists a voice in the decision. It was not just that they did not want to send their money to England. They believed in democracy. Democracy means "rule by the people," and the colonists believed that Britain should ask for their approval before it took their money.

The foundation of democracy is a belief in the value of the individual. Every person is important and everyone has a right to make decisions for themselves. Each individual cannot decide matters that affect the whole society, of course. But every citizen should have a say in the decision.

These democratic ideals were laid out in the

Declaration of Independence, which was passed by the Continental Congress on July 4, 1776. That document's vision of the purpose of government still inspires people around the world today:

> We hold these truths to be self-evident, that all men are created equal, that they are endowed by their Creator with certain unalienable Rights, that among these are Life, Liberty, and the Pursuit of Happiness. That, to secure these Rights, Governments are instituted among Men, deriving their just powers from the consent of the governed.[1]

The founders of the United States were determined that the just powers of that government would depend on the ongoing consent of the people it would govern. The people needed not only a way to give their consent in the first place, but to withdraw their consent if they did not like what the government did in the future.

How were the people to express their consent, or lack of it? The answer they came up with was a congress—a meeting of people from around the country. Together, they would discuss the issues of the day and make the laws and other decisions that had to be made.

Not everyone could attend such a congress, however. There were vast distances to travel. Besides most people had their own jobs to do, and families to look after. They did not have the time or the money to travel to some distant place whenever the congress met. And, even if they did, there were far too many of them to gather in one place. The number who actually attended the congress would obviously have to be limited. But those who came would not speak only for themselves. They would represent all the other people back home who could not be there.

If they were to represent their fellow citizens, they would have to be chosen by them. This would give them the right to speak for their fellow citizens, and make decisions in their name.

▶ The First Congresses

Representative government was not a new idea, even in 1776. Forms of it had existed at least as long ago as ancient Greece and Rome. Our mother country, England, had an elected parliament, which had more power—in many ways—than the British king. And some Native American tribes were electing their leaders long before the British ever arrived in North America.

Virginia, the first permanent British settlement in North America, elected representatives to a general assembly in 1619. This eventually evolved into a two-house legislature. By the time of the American Revolution, Virginia had already had more than one hundred and fifty years of representative government. The other colonies had representative bodies of their own as well.

The first important congress—or meeting—of delegates from several colonies took place in New York's City Hall in the cold month of October 1765. Representatives of nine of the colonies came together in a meeting inspired by the Virginia House of

Burgesses. They were there to protest the Stamp Act, which imposed an English tax on all American newspapers, legal documents, and other printed materials. Congress petitioned the British Parliament to repeal this hated act, which it eventually did.

▶ The Continental Congresses

A decade later representatives from the colonies came together again. This time the meeting was in Philadelphia. Fifty-five delegates, from all the colonies—except Georgia, Ontario, and Quebec—crowded into Carpenter's Hall on September 5, 1774. It was the first of many sessions, which would continue for almost two months, of the First Continental Congress.

Like the Stamp Act congress before it, the gathering was not a legislative body. It passed no laws. But it did claim to represent the people of the colonies, and it petitioned the British Parliament in their name.

It was a remarkable gathering, and at least one member knew it. "The Congress," wrote John Adams, "is such an assembly as never before came together, *on a sudden*, in any part of the world. Here are fortunes, abilities, learning, eloquence, acuteness equal to any I ever met with in my life."[2]

Besides John Adams, the delegates to this historic congress included two more future Presidents of the United States, George Washington and Thomas Jefferson. Patrick Henry of Virginia was there as well, along with John and Edward Rutledge of South

∇∧∇∧∇∧∇∧∇∧∇∧∇∧∇∧∇∧∇∧∇∧∇∧∇∧∇∧∇∧∇∧∇∧∇∧∇∧∇

Carolina, and John Adams's cousin, Samuel, from Massachusetts.

A Second Continental Congress met on May 10, 1775. By that time the British Parliament had turned down the petition from the First Continental Congress, and there had been violence between colonists and British troops at Lexington and Concord.

Although most representatives hoped they could find a way to win liberty for themselves without more bloodshed and a total break with Britain, the Congress directed George Washington to organize a colonial army, just in case.

In the meantime the Second Continental Congress became a real governing body. It ordered the printing of paper money, made rules for trade with the colonies, and even sent delegates to foreign countries to ask their help.

On July 2, 1776, the representatives voted to break all ties with England, and on July 4 the delegates passed the Declaration of Independence, spelling out their reasons for the break. The Second Continental Congress continued to meet until December, when it was replaced by a new assembly known as the Third Continental Congress. This was the congress that passed the Articles of Confederation—the first blueprint for the American government—in 1777.

The Articles were sent to the states for their approval that same year. All the states had to agree before the Articles could go into effect. Twelve of the thirteen states ratified the Articles quickly, but

Maryland refused to go along. This meant, among other things, that the Congress of the Confederation could not meet. As a result the Third Continental Congress continued to direct the fight for independence.

Stubborn Maryland finally agreed to the Articles in 1781. On March 1 of that year the Third Continental Congress was formally disbanded, to be replaced by still another body—the Congress of the Confederation. It was this congress that made peace with Great Britain in the Treaty of Paris and ran the federal government for the first seven years of the new nation's existence.

▶ The Congress of the Confederation

The Congress of the Confederation *was* the federal government. There was no national court system and no executive branch of government at all. This would seem to make Congress a very powerful body. In reality, however, most of the real power rested with the governments of the thirteen original states.

The national Congress had only one house. Its members were not elected directly but by the state legislatures. Some state delegations had two members, while some had as many as seven. No matter how many members it had, however—and no matter how many people there were in the state it represented—each state delegation got only one vote in Congress.

Not content with picking the delegates in the first place, the states kept power over their actions. They paid their salaries and had the right to remove or replace them at any time. Everything Congress wanted to do had to be approved by at least nine of the state delegations before it could actually go into effect. What's more, although Congress could pass laws, it had no way to make the states obey them.

▶ Conflict over Confederation

Some influential Americans—including Alexander Hamilton and James Madison—were troubled by the weakness of the Congress of the Confederation. They called for a convention to be held in Philadelphia in 1787 to re-examine the Articles and to amend them.

Other Americans, however, liked the Articles of Confederation just the way there were. They distrusted the Congress and wanted to keep it as weak as possible. Among them, oddly enough, were many members of Congress itself. They feared what a convention might do, and for as long as they could, they kept the Congress from endorsing such a meeting. But trouble was stirring in the countryside—trouble that would scare people and reveal the central government's lack of real power.

▶ Shays' Rebellion

Farmers in several states were having a hard time in the 1780s. Many were threatened with the loss of their farms and their livelihood. Bad harvests and poor markets for their crops made them unable to pay their taxes and meet their mortgage payments. Some of the hard-pressed farmers took up their rifles to resist the local tax collectors who came to drive them off their farms.

In Massachusetts a group of desperate farmers banded together under the leadership of an ex-captain in the American Revolution, Daniel Shays. Feeling the strength of weapons and numbers, they stood up to local officials and merchants, and even stormed the government arsenal at Springfield, Massachusetts. The Massachusetts state militia managed to rout the rebels in battle, but many of the farmers escaped into neighboring states. The central government was helpless to do anything about it.

"Shays' Rebellion" showed the weakness of the central government. Congress was virtually powerless to help Massachusetts or any of the other states troubled by angry farmers. What if more rebellions occurred? Was the new country going to be defenseless against its own citizens? Was anarchy free to triumph?

Shays' Rebellion gave new life to the call for a Philadelphia Convention. The revolutionary hero George Washington had always wanted a stronger central government, but now he was convinced it was necessary. For him the rebellion was an attack on private property. "Our government must be braced, changed, or altered to secure our lives and property," he wrote. "I feel infinitely more than I can express for the disorders which have arisen. Good God!"[3]

Even Congress finally gave its half-hearted approval, although most representatives wanted the convention to confine itself to amending the Articles.

They did not want to see the system of government changed altogether.

▶ Inventing The United States Congress

Twelve states sent delegates to the convention. Only Rhode Island chose not to attend. Although more than seventy delegates were picked, only fifty-five ever attended. Among them were James Madison, Benjamin Franklin, Alexander Hamilton, along with many lesser known but important delegates. They

The inside of the Capitol dome. A Latin inscription on the banner in the painting means, "out of many, one." It is a good description of the great task of the United States Congress.

chose George Washington as president of the convention.

In the end these men—and all of them were men, because only men were allowed to participate in political affairs in those days—decided to throw out the Articles of Confederation altogether. In its place they wrote a whole new document they called the Constitution of the United States.

The United States Constitution was ratified and went into effect in 1789. This is the document that invented the Congress of the United States that exists today. Together with the amendments that have been added over the past two centuries, the Constitution remains the blueprint for the federal government—and therefore, for the Congress.

The First of Three Branches

The Constitution gave the federal government much more power than the Congress of the Confederation ever had. But where the Congress had held almost all the federal power under the Articles, the new Constitution divided power between three separate branches of government. Now, in addition to the Congress, there would be a judicial branch, and an executive branch run by a President.

▶ Checks and Balances

Congress was—and still is—one part of a great system of checks and balances that helps protect the country from dictatorship. The writers of the Constitution spread the powers of government among three branches in order to keep any one branch of the government from getting too powerful.

The Constitution gives each branch different jobs to do. Although different, the jobs tend to overlap in many ways. This assures that each of the three branches will keep the others from getting out of hand. The main powers and duties granted to these three branches in 1789 remain with them today. In some ways, however, they have been expanded.

The President is the head of the executive branch of the United States government. The Constitution gives the President three main responsibilities. The first is to run the foreign policy of the country. The second is to oversee the operations of the federal government. The third is to enforce the nation's laws.

The President also has some legislative powers. He or she can propose legislation to the Congress, and can choose to sign or to veto bills passed by it. If the President vetoes (or disapproves) a bill, it cannot go into effect unless Congress overrides the veto. This can be done by a two-thirds vote of both houses of Congress.

The judicial branch of the federal government, meanwhile, has the job of interpreting the laws. It consists of the Supreme Court and the other federal courts. Among them, they have the duty to decide cases involving a wide range of legal issues, including possible violations of federal laws; legal disputes between states, or between United States citizens and foreign citizens or governments; treaties with foreign nations; and "all cases affecting ambassadors, other public ministers, and consuls."[1] The Supreme Court also has the power to decide cases involving rights protected by the United States Constitution.[2]

▶ "... A Congress of the United States ..."

The President and the courts are vital to the United States system of government. But in the minds of the men who invented this new form of government, the Congress came first.

Congress even comes first in the Constitution of the United States. It is given its power by the very first Article of the Constitution, which declares that:

This daguerreotype, taken by John Plumbe around 1846, is the earliest known photograph of the Capitol.

"All legislative powers herein granted shall be vested in a Congress of the United States which shall consist of a Senate and House of Representatives."[3]

The members of the House of Representatives, the Constitution proclaimed, were to be "chosen every second Year by the People of the several States,"[4] while the two senators from each state would be "chosen by the Legislature thereof."[5]

The representatives and senators would act in the people's name, and—of course—with the people's consent. If the people did not like what their representatives were doing, they could vote them out of office when their two years were up. If people did not like what their senators did, their elected state legislatures could remove them as well. Removing a senator would take longer, however. Except for those named to fill out an unfinished term, senators served for six years instead of two.

Senators still serve for six-year terms, although they are no longer picked by state legislatures. Since Amendment XVII was ratified in 1913, they have been elected directly by the people, just as House members are.

▶ Duties and Powers

Each state and locality makes it own laws that apply to people and institutions inside its borders, but Congress makes the laws that apply to everyone in the country. Congress also makes the laws that control business and other dealings that cross state borders; as well as dealings between the states and the federal government, and relationships with foreign nations.

Most of the responsibilities of Congress are spelled out in Section VIII of Article I of the Constitution. Among them:

> The Congress shall have Power to lay and collect taxes . . . [and] to pay the Debts and provide for the common Defense and general Welfare of the United States;
>
> To borrow Money on the Credit of the United States;
>
> To regulate Commerce with foreign Nations, and among the several States, and with the Indian Tribes . . .
>
> To coin Money, regulate the Value thereof . . .
>
> To establish Post Offices and post Roads . . .
>
> To constitute Tribunals inferior to the supreme Court;
>
> To define and punish . . . offenses against the Law of Nations;
>
> To declare War . . . To raise and support Armies . . .
>
> To provide for calling forth the Militia to execute the Laws of the Union, suppress Insurrections and repel Invasions;
>
> To provide for organizing, arming, and disciplining, the Militia . . .
>
> —And
>
> To make all Laws which shall be necessary and proper for carrying into Execution the foregoing Powers, and all other Powers vested by this Constitution in the Government of the United States, or in any Department or Officer thereof.[6]

Other parts of the Constitution grant more specific powers to Congress. These include the power "to declare the punishment of Treason"[7]; to regulate elections for federal office; to make rules regulating "the Territory or other Property" of the United States;[8] and to accept or reject the admission of new states into the Union.[9]

As the Watergate scandal showed, Congress also has the sole power of impeachment.[10] Only Congress has the right to charge and try the President of the United States and other high federal officials for official crimes—the right that would allow Congress, in effect, to force President Nixon to resign from office almost two centuries later.

One of the most important powers granted to Congress by the Constitution was to amend the Constitution itself. Like several other important powers, however, this one is shared. Although Congress can pass a Constitutional amendment, three-fourths of the states have to agree before it can go into effect.[11] Two-thirds of the states can also call on Congress to hold a Constitutional convention, which would be able to rewrite the Constitution altogether.

Each house of Congress also has certain powers of its own. The House of Representatives, for example, has the right to decide presidential elections deadlocked in the electoral college.[12] The Senate has the right to advise and consent on the naming of important executive and judicial officials and on treaties with foreign governments.[13]

▶ The War Power

Of all the powers listed in the Constitution, by far the most awesome is the power to declare war. The President is the Commander in Chief of the Army and Navy, but the Constitution says he or she needs the Congress before committing the full force of American military power to war.

At one time it was assumed that Congress had to pass an actual declaration of war before United States troops could be sent into battle, except in self-defense. This is what Congress did in World War I (1914–1918) and World War II (1939–1945), for example.

In recent years, however, Congress has allowed troops to be sent into action without declaring war. Even the long war in Vietnam (1959–1975) was never actually declared by Congress. Critics of recent Congresses complain that Congress has all but given up its power to declare war to the President.[14]

Some members of Congress respond that they have not given up the power. They just express it in other ways. They are content to let the President make the initial decision to use military force, because he can respond more quickly to emergencies. Congress can then show that it approves—or disapproves by voting for or against money to pay for ongoing military action. The war power, they say, remains in the Constitution, and can be used whenever Congress has the will to do it.

▶ "Necessary and Proper"

The members of the House and Senate have lots of responsibilities, but the Constitution makes clear that their main job is to write laws—"all Laws . . . necessary and proper" for Congress to do the many jobs the Constitution gives it to do.[15]

Congress has used this clause to perform various acts not specifically listed among its powers in the Constitution. Very early in the country's history, for instance, Congress established a national bank. Some people protested that the Constitution did not give Congress the right to establish a national bank. Congress had no right to act in areas that the Constitution did not say it could. Under the system of checks and balances, it was up to the United States Supreme Court to decide.

In 1819 a unanimous Supreme Court ruled that the "necessary and proper" clause implies that Congress can act in ways that are not spelled out in the Constitution. "Let the end be legitimate," declared Chief Justice John Marshall in the case of *McCulloch v. Maryland*, "and all means which are appropriate [and] which are not prohibited . . . are constitutional," he declared.[16]

▶ All Laws?

"All Laws" does not mean *all* the laws of the country, of course. It only includes the laws that are necessary for Congress to fulfill its responsibilities. There are many laws besides those passed by Congress. Every state and local government has laws of its own.

Most civil laws, in fact, are actually written by the state legislatures. They are designed to meet the special concerns and situations that exist within each state, and they vary from state to state. The laws that say at which age people can marry without their parents' consent is one example. A fifteen-year-old girl can legally get married in Mississippi, but nowhere else in the United States.

Most criminal laws are also state laws. What is a crime in one state may be perfectly legal in another. Punishments vary too. Almost three-quarters of the states have the power to inflict the death penalty, for example, but the rest do not.

So why does Congress make laws at all? And what makes the laws Congress passes different from other laws? The key to answering these questions is found in the word *uniform*, which is used three times in Section VIII of Article I.

Congress makes those laws that apply to *everyone* in the United States, and not just to people within a certain state.

▶ The Power of the Purse

Perhaps the most vital of all Congress's powers is the "power of the purse." As we have seen Congress is the branch of government that sets and collects taxes; and it is Congress that has the right to coin, borrow, and spend money for the United States.

Bills that raise money have to be introduced first in the House. This includes all bills that call for the raising or spending of money. The Senate, however, can propose amendments to money bills, and both houses have to agree before the bills can become law.[17]

Although Congress has the Constitutional power to write and pass a federal budget, the President plays an important role in the process. This is especially true when the President's party has a large majority in Congress. At those times Congress is more likely to follow the President's lead.

The President was given a central role in budget-making by the Congress itself, in the 1921 Budget and Accounting Act.[18]

Each year the President submits a budget to Congress. The Congress is then free to change the proposal or to throw it out altogether and write a budget of its own.

This control over the government's purse strings is the key to Congress's role in the system of checks and balances. Money is needed for everything that any branch of government might want to do, from hiring a new federal judge to sweeping the floors in the White House. The fact that Congress controls the purse strings gives it influence over everything the government does. If Congress dislikes some activity of the executive or judicial branch, it can always threaten to cut off the money for it.

The power of the purse extends beyond the government. It gives Congress an enormous influence over the whole economy. By raising or lowering taxes, Congress can increase or reduce economic activity throughout society. The more money Congress takes from people in taxes, the less they have to spend on clothes, food, and other goods. On the other hand, the more money that Congress spends inside the country, the more money businesses make and the more jobs they can provide.

▶ Oversight

There are scores—if not hundreds—of federal departments, bureaus, commissions, and other agencies. This vast complex, known as the federal bureaucracy, performs most of the day-to-day work of government. Most of these agencies are in the executive branch, but Congress has a role to play in overseeing what they do, and how they do it.

In fact, Congress has several roles. It is Congress that sets the budgets of most of these agencies, and Congress that makes the laws that the agencies have to enforce. What's more, Congress keeps track of the agencies' activities, making sure they are doing their jobs and that they are not overstepping their bounds.

This power—known as the power of oversight—allows Congress to be a watchdog over virtually every aspect of the federal government. It was this power that the Senate used to set up the Watergate Committee and expose the misdeeds of the White House to the nation.

▶ Limits on Congressional Power

The powers the Constitution gives to Congress are great, but they are not total. Just as Congress acts as a brake on the executive and judicial branches, those branches act as a brake on Congress. So do a number of Constitutional amendments, passed by generations of Americans concerned with the rights of individuals and the rights of the states.

Even as it was first written, the Constitution seemed to confine Congress's power to the areas spelled out in Article I. Article II specifically forbade Congress to perform certain other acts, and ten amendments—known as the Bill of Rights—were soon added, which restricted the power of Congress even further. Other amendments limiting federal power have been passed since.

The very first amendment declares that "Congress shall make no law" restricting the freedom of religion, speech, press, free assembly, or the people's right to appeal to the government.[19] Other specific rights are protected from Congressional action by the next eight amendments. Amendment X offers a more sweeping protection. It declares the powers not granted to federal government by the Constitution "are reserved to the States . . . or to the people."[20]

▶ A Menace or a Protection?

The Bill of Rights treats Congress as a potential menace to individual rights and to the rights of the states. That is why some of the amendments specifically command that Congress "make no law" restricting such rights.

Some of the later amendments, however, assume just the opposite. These amendments see Congress as the protector of the people's rights. For that reason, they expand Congress's power. Section I of Amendment XIII outlaws slavery. Section II specifically gives Congress the "power to enforce this article by appropriate legislation."[21] Several other amendments—including XI, XIV, XIX, XXIII, and XXVI—have similar sections that grant Congress the power to pass more laws.

Which assumption is correct? Is Congress a threat to the rights of the people or is it a protector of their rights? The answer, as implied by the Constitution, is that it is both.

▶ Changes

Congress has gone through many changes over the years. Both the House and the Senate have gotten much larger than they were when they were formed, and they meet more often than they did then.

The powers of Congress have also expanded, along with the powers of the federal government as a whole. And the jobs of representatives and senators have gotten more and more complex.

But, in most essential ways, today's Congress is the same institution that was established by the Constitution more than two centuries ago.

Making Democracy Work

Congress is a way of making democracy work. In theory, Congress itself is a democratic body. Every senator is equal to every other senator. Every representative is equal to every other representative. And every member of Congress gets one vote.

In practice, however, some senators and congresspersons are more important than others. Congress is a large and complex institution, made up of two bodies, each of which has its own rules and ways of getting their jobs done. No institution as large and complex as Congress could run without leadership.

▶ The Leadership

Both the House and the Senate have specific leadership positions, to which members are either

34

elected or appointed. Some are Constitutional. The Constitution requires the House to have a speaker, for example, and for the Senate to have a president and president *pro tempore* (or temporary president). These are the officials who preside over the sessions of the two bodies.

The speaker of the House is elected by the representatives from among their own members. Because one political party usually dominates the House, the speaker is inevitably chosen by the members of that majority party. For most of the last half century, the speaker of the House was a Democrat. Since the congressional session of 1994, however, the speaker has been a Republican.

Although the Constitution does not give him or her any special powers, the speaker of the House is perhaps the most powerful single person in Congress. This is because the rules of the House give him or her virtual control of many House activities.

On the other hand, the president of the Senate has very little actual power. He or she is not even a senator. The Constitution dictates that he or she must be the Vice President of the United States. Not being a senator, he or she does not even vote— except when there is a tie among the voting senators. In that case, this non-senator's vote becomes the most important vote of all—the one that decides whether the measure passes or fails.

Because the Vice President is likely to be busy elsewhere, and may even have to take over the duties of President, the senators pick a president *pro tempore*. He or she presides over the Senate when the Vice President is busy or has to assume the office of President of the United States.

The speaker of the House appoints another member to preside over the House whenever he or she is too busy. This is almost invariably a member of his or her own party. When the Republican minority leader Bob Michel retired in 1992, after more than thirty years in the minority, the Democratic Speaker of the House Tom Foley appointed him to preside briefly over a final session. It was a special honor to a man who had hoped to become House speaker himself some day.

▶ Other Officers

The Constitution also gives each body the right to "chuse [sic] their other Officers" as they see fit.[1] In practice these positions tend to be partisan. That is they tend to be as much party offices as Congressional ones.

The members of the majority party in each house pick a majority leader, and the members of the minority party pick a minority leader. Because the speaker is the true head of the majority party in the House, the majority leader's role is really that of a deputy leader. In addition, the parties in each body select assistants, called the majority and minority whips, to help plan and organize their activities.

Besides their duties in Congress, these officers are spokespersons for their parties and for the Congress. They are responsible for communicating with

Perhaps the most powerful of all Senate majority leaders, Lyndon Johnson became Vice President in 1961, and President in 1963

each other, with the other body of Congress, with the President, and with the public at large.

Other important leaders in Congress include the chairpersons of the committees and subcommittees as well as the officials of several party organizations.

▶ Committees and Subcommittees

As many as two thousand bills come before Congress each year, sometimes more. There is no way for the entire House and Senate to carefully consider each one of them, so each body divides itself into smaller committees and subcommittees. Even these committees can only give limited attention to most bills that come before them.

Committees are where most of the real debate—and the real work—of Congress is done. The committee "marks up" the bill—writing the final version that will be submitted to the whole body of the House or Senate. If the committee decides that the bill is not worthwhile, it can vote the bill down or table it. Tabling a bill means to postpone a vote on it. Most tabled bills die because they are never voted on by the whole House or Senate.

Each committee has it own area of interest. The Agricultural Committees of each house, for example, are concerned with issues important to farmers. The Armed Services Committees specialize in military matters. Bills affecting the interests of each committee are referred to that committee before they are brought to the floor of the House or Senate.

There are different kinds of committees. Each house has some more or less permanent standing committees, like the committees on appropriations, which mark up all money-raising measures. There are also joint committees that include members from both houses. Each house also has select committees, often appointed by the leadership of the house to handle investigations.

The power to investigate is not specifically granted by the Constitution, but it is implied. If Congress is supposed to make laws affecting social and economic affairs, it must be able to collect information about those issues. If Congress is to oversee the doings of government agencies, it must have some way to find out what they are doing.

Most committees are divided up into subcommittees, each of which deals with a smaller area of interest within the broader concerns of the committee. The House Committee on Foreign Affairs, for example, has nine subcommittees. They include subcommittees on Africa; Arms Control; International Security and Science; Asian and Pacific Affairs; Europe and the Middle East; Human Rights and International Organizations; International Economic Policy and Trade; International Operations; and Western Hemisphere Affairs.

▶ Committee Membership

Like Congress itself, committees are partisan bodies. They reflect the party divisions of the body as a whole. If Republicans make up 75 percent of representatives, they will get three out of four seats on most House committees. The House and Senate ethics committees are exceptions to this rule. They have equal numbers of Democrats and Republicans.

Members are usually appointed to committees by the party leadership in the body. The Republicans in the House even have a Committee on Committees to make these decisions. Which committee someone gets on can be very important. A senator from a farm state, for example, wants to be on the Agriculture Committee, where he or she can help the farmers back home. A House member whose district has several aerospace industries wants to be on the Science, Space, and Technology Committee.

Some standing committees are tremendously powerful. The Committees on Appropriations have the most to say about how much money will be raised and spent by the federal government. The House Ways and Means and House Rules Committees have a kind of general jurisdiction over virtually every measure that comes before the House. The Rules Committee, for example, sets the limits of debate on every bill that comes to the floor. It even decides in advance which amendments can be voted on. This gives the members of these committees life-and-death power over many bills. Being on one of these major committees automatically makes a senator or representative one of the more important members of Congress.

Committee chairpersons are chosen by the members of their committee. These officers are not as powerful as they used to be. A few decades ago a chair could virtually dictate what a committee would do. Nowadays younger senators and representatives are more independent. They are likely to resent it when a chair becomes too bossy and refuses to go along with him or her. Nonetheless, chairs remain extremely influential in the way committees—and therefore Congress—do business.

It is not easy to get a majority of members to agree on anything as complicated as the average bill. Committees are where many of the compromises needed to get a bill through are worked out—and in a democracy those compromises are necessary if anything is going to get done.

▶ Passing a Bill

Once a bill comes out of committee, it goes to the floor of the House or the Senate. The full body then either passes the bill, rejects it, or amends it.

Before either house can vote on any measure, there has to be quorum present—the minimum number of members in order to do business. In the House a quorum is a majority of the total number of members, plus one. In 1995 the House had 435 members, which meant that 219 members had to be present for a vote to be taken.

Most measures only need a majority of those present and voting to pass. This means a bill can pass either house without an actual majority of the members voting for it. In the House, for example, where 219 members make a quorum, a measure could pass with as few as 110 votes.

There are exceptions to the majority rule. It takes a two thirds vote in each house to pass a

The opening of the 32nd. Congress, as depicted in the Illustrated News *in 1853.*

Constitutional amendment, for example, or to override a presidential veto.

Ordinarily members of both houses declare which way they vote on each bill by punching their vote into an electronic voting machine. If they are present, but do not want to vote either yes or no, they are recorded as abstaining from the vote.

Not every vote is recorded. Measures that no one is opposed to—known as "noncontroversial" bills—can be passed by unanimous consent, without any individual senator or congressperson actually casting a vote.

▶ Working Together

Just as the three branches of government check and balance each other, so do the two bodies of

Congress. In order to become law, bills have to pass *both* the House and the Senate.

Except for money-raising measures, which have to start out in the House, bills can be introduced in either house. After a bill is passed in the house that gave birth to it, it goes to the other body. If it passes there, too, it goes to the President to be signed into law. If it fails to pass in either house, it dies.

Because each body works on the bill separately, the House and Senate often pass different versions of the same bill. So which version of the bill becomes law? Most often the answer is neither one.

What usually happens is that both versions of the bill are sent to a conference, or meeting, made up of several members from each house. These conference committees can be almost any size. Most are fairly small, but at least one—the one that dealt with the 1993 budget bill—had 228 members!

The Conference Committee reconciles the two bills. In effect, it comes up with a *third* version of the bill, a compromise the conference members hope that both houses can accept. This "conference report" is then voted on by both houses. Then, if—and only if—it passes in both houses, it is sent on to the President to sign into law.

▶ Vetoes and Overrides

The President is not required to sign every bill Congress sends to him or her. What happens if the President simply fails to sign the bill depends on where the Congress is in its schedule. If Congress ends its session within ten days of the President refusing to sign the bill, it dies. This is called a "pocket veto," because it is as if the President put the bill in a pocket to keep the Congress from acting on it again. But if Congress *is* still in session ten days after the President received the bill, it becomes law anyway. This allows the President to let Congress have its way without giving his or her approval to what it has done.

The President's other option is to veto the bill outright. That is, to send it back to Congress with a written declaration that he or she opposes the bill and refuses to accept it. This kills the bill, unless Congress overrides the veto by a two-thirds vote of each house.

This is much harder than getting a simple majority to pass a bill in the first place. First of all, it is hard to get two-thirds of both houses to agree on anything, particularly something controversial enough to be opposed by the President. What's more, many members of the President's party are reluctant to override a veto, even if they like the bill. Voting to override a veto—not just voting *for* the bill—is like voting *against* the President.

Just how hard overriding a veto can be is shown by the record of President Franklin D. Roosevelt. Of the 635 bills he vetoed from 1933 to 1945, Congress managed to override only 9. Hard or not, Congress has the power to override the President if it wants to do so. It always has the last word when it comes to passing legislation.

An Exclusive Club

The two bodies of Congress are very different. The Senate is often compared to a kind of select club, with its own rules and traditions. At any given time there are only one hundred senators for the entire country.

The Constitutional requirements to be a senator are not lengthy, however; there are only three. A senator must be at least thirty years old, must have been a citizen of the United States for at least nine years, and must be a resident of the state from which he or she is elected.[1]

The exclusiveness comes from the fact that only two people can become senators from each state. It does not matter how big the state is, nor how many people live there. Wyoming's 470,242 residents are represented by two senators, as are California's

31,210,750.[2] And since each Senate term runs for six years, seats in the Senate do not open up very often. Only thirty-three or thirty-four seats ever come up for election at one time. Many of those are won by sitting senators who get re-elected. This means that an even smaller number of new people enter the Senate every two years.

▶ Representing the States

The writers of the United States Constitution named the Senate after the law-making body of the Roman Republic. The senators of ancient Rome were among the Republic's most distinguished citizens. They were appointed to their office by government officials called censors, and were expected to uphold traditional values and to keep Roman society stable and prosperous.

The first United States senators were also appointed to office, but by the legislatures of their states. In a sense they did not represent the people, as such, but the states. Also like the Roman senators, they were expected to uphold traditional values. The framers of the Constitution were afraid that the elected members of the House might be too rash and radical. They wanted a more careful Senate to act as a brake on the House if it tried to go too far.

Even while launching their great experiment in democracy, many of the nation's founders did not fully trust the people. They worried that the ordinary voters might elect representatives who were too much like themselves. That is, people who were relatively uneducated and had little property—who had no real stake in an orderly society.

Most of the founders were men of property and social position themselves. They wanted senators with property of their own to protect, who would be careful to protect the property of others. State legislatures, they hoped, would be more likely to pick such representatives than the voters would.

This way of picking senators lasted for more than a century. Since 1913, however, senators have been elected directly, just as House members are. More than eighty years later, however, senators still tend to have more money and property than House members.

▶ "Watching Paint Dry"

Running for the Senate costs much more money than running for the House. House candidates only have to campaign in one district. Senate hopefuls have to campaign over an entire state.

Senators make the same basic salary as House members—$133,600 in 1995—but they are more pampered on the job. Each body makes its own rules, and the rules of the Senate are more relaxed than those of the House.

People who prefer the way the Senate acts say that it is more stately than the House. Critics say that it is more dull and stodgy. "The House is more raucous," admits Barry R. Jackson, a staff member of the House Republican conference. "The Senate is about as exciting as watching paint dry."[3]

The different tradition of the two houses is

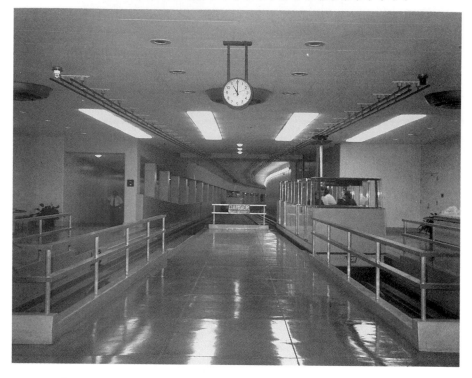

An underground rail system transports representatives, senators, staffers, and tourists between the Capitol and other congressional office buildings.

shown in the more courtly manner in which senators speak to each other in public. Even bitter opponents will address each other as "my good friend" and praise each other for "dedicated service" before launching into a partisan attack.

In private, however, behavior is often very different. At one time most senators did treat each other as fellow members of a club. Whether Democrat, Republican, or independent, they were all senators. While they might detest each other's policies, they sought each other's company. Today, however, political disagreements very often reflect personal dislikes as well.

"There used to be friendships [between Democrats and Republicans] in the Senate," mourned retiring Senator David Boren of Oklahoma in 1994. But "that's broken down."[4]

▶ The Filibuster

The most obvious difference between the rules of the two bodies is the Senate filibuster. Because the House has 435 members, it has to put strict limits on debate. If every member could speak for hours on every bill, nothing would ever get done. Even if only a small percentage of representatives wanted to speak at length on a bill, debate could go on for weeks. For this reason the time allowed for debate on a bill is strictly limited. What's more, it is set in advance, before debate ever begins.

The Senate, on the other hand, has only one hundred members and can be more generous with its time. Under Senate rules the time for debate on a bill is unlimited. It can only be restricted if everyone agrees to limit it.

Traditionally the time each senator can speak is unlimited as well. Whenever a member is "recognized" to speak in either house, he or she "has the floor." That means that he or she is the only one who is free to talk. In the House each speaker is only given the floor for a specific amount of time. In the Senate each speaker has the floor for as long as he or she wants to keep it.

This gives individual senators an enormous

amount of power. If opponents of a bill that most senators favor can get the floor, they can delay voting on the bill for as long as they can keep talking. This tactic, known as a filibuster, can prevent action for an indefinite amount of time. If a number of opponents can get the floor, one after the other, they can tie up the Senate for days.

Eventually something has to give. If the majority of senators are determined to pass the bill, the filibusterer will finally have to give up and surrender the floor. If nothing else, he or she will fall asleep. But when the Senate is busy or wants to end a session and get home, the majority sometimes gives up first and decides not to vote on the bill at all.

The filibuster is controversial. It can be seen as the last resort a minority has to keep from being stampeded by the majority. It allows cooler heads to prevent reckless action in an emotional response to a crisis. By forcing the Senate to take its time, a filibuster can sometimes force compromise, and result in a better bill. This view of the filibuster was seen in the classic movie *Mr. Smith Goes to Washington*. In that film a valiant young senator, played by Jimmy Stewart, used a filibuster to expose political corruption.

However, the filibuster got a bad reputation among many Americans when white senators from the South used it to block civil rights measures in the 1930s, 1940s, and 1950s. In 1938, for example, a group of southerners filibustered for twenty-nine days against a bill to give the federal government power to combat lynching.[5]

The filibuster is a tool that can be used by anyone. There is nothing either liberal or conservative about it. Senators of all political stripes have used it for all sorts of purposes. Senator Wayne Morse of Wyoming, for instance, once spoke for twenty-two hours and twenty-six minutes in an effort to block a bill dealing with off-shore oil drilling.[6]

The filibuster is being used more now than ever before. The Senate was faced with no less than four separate filibusters on what was scheduled to be the last day of the 103rd Congress.[7] At the same time it is getting easier to end a filibuster. At any time sixty senators can vote to "invoke cloture"; that is, to close debate and end a filibuster. The tradition of unlimited freedom is strong, however, and many senators are reluctant to vote for cloture. Young senators are less tied to tradition, however, and more willing to invoke cloture.

Some critics want to see the filibuster outlawed altogether. They consider it an insult to democracy. After all, if the majority of senators want a bill, should they not be allowed to pass it?

The People's House

If the Senate was designed to represent the most stable and conservative forces of society, the House was intended to represent ordinary citizens. For that reason it is often called "the people's House."

▶ A President in the House

The House may be the least exclusive of the two bodies of Congress, but it is the only one ever to have an ex-President as a member. John Quincy Adams, who had been both a senator and secretary of state before becoming President, won election to the House in 1830, two years after losing a bid for re-election as President.

A fine speaker and a stubborn champion of whatever he believed in, Adams became one of the greatest representatives of all time. He is best known for his fight to get rid of the House "gag rule." This was a rule that denied members the chance to debate specific issues.

Adams bitterly fought the gag rule for eight years, speaking against it so powerfully that he was nicknamed "Old Man Eloquent." Finally, in 1844, the House voted to do away with the gag rule and take up the slavery petitions. Adams was still a representative in 1848, when he collapsed of a stroke on the House floor and died two days later.

▶ Differences from the Senate

Both houses of Congress represent the same citizens of the United States, but they represent them in different ways. Most, if not all, of these differences make the House members more responsive to the individuals they serve.

There are more than four times as many members of the House as senators. Each senator represents all the people of his or her entire state, while each House member represents the people of his or her congressional district. There are roughly five hundred seventy thousand Americans for every congressperson, compared to roughly 2.5 million for every senator. This means that each member of the House represents a smaller number of people—known as constituents—than each senator. This is still a high figure compared to many other democracies. In the United Kingdom, for instance, each member of Parliament represents about eighty-eight thousand five hundred citizens.

During his long and distinguished career in the House after leaving the presidency, John Quincy Adams earned the nickname "Old Man Eloquent."

Even so, with fewer people to serve than senators, House members can actually meet a higher proportion of them. They can listen to their concerns and respond to their needs. This can make a big difference in the relationship between representatives and their constituents. An individual citizen who needs help in dealing with the federal government is more likely to receive it from a House member. Because the House member has fewer constituents competing for his or her attention, the representative is more likely to take the time to listen to the constituent's concerns.

Because representatives only serve for two years, they have to win the voters' approval three times as often as senators. One effect of this is that they are almost constantly running for office. This makes them even more sensitive to the concerns of voters than senators are; but it can also make them more timid. House members are even more worried about doing something that might upset voters. They know that they will have to go back and be elected by those voters very soon, and people who are angry at what they do will have less time to forget.

For all these reasons constituents often feel closer to their representatives than to their senators. House members, in turn, seem to feel closer to their constituents.

▶ House Debate

Debate in the House is very different from debate in the Senate. Senators speak from their places on the floor. Representatives come to the front of the

House chamber and stand at one of two podiums facing the other members. In the Senate there are few limits on debate. In the House there are many.

Each side in a House debate is usually given an equal amount of the allotted time to make its arguments. Each side's time may be used in a block or the sides may take turns. Sometimes, a member will ask a speaker on the other side to "yield" to him or her for a question or a response.

Control over each side's time is given to one member from that side. This is usually someone who has a strong interest in the bill and who has played a major role in either writing or opposing it. He or she divides up the time among the members, yielding time to the others who want to speak for that side.

When both sides are finished, the vote is taken. There are two kinds of votes. In a voice vote all in favor of a bill call out "Aye" together, then all those opposed call "Nay." When the winning side is obvious, a voice vote may be enough. But any member can call for a recorded vote. If "a sufficient number" of members present agree, a recorded vote is ordered.

At one time, a voice roll call was used to record the votes of representatives. Today such votes are "taken by electronic device."

▶ One-Minutes and Special Orders

The House has several practices that make up, in part, for the limitations on floor debate. These practices act as bookends for the Congressional day. The first is a recent addition to the House schedule, known as the morning hour.

At the start of business each day the House is in session, a number of individual members are recognized to speak for one minute on any subject they want. This allows representatives to publicly proclaim their positions on an upcoming bill, or to give credit to constituents who have distinguished themselves in some way.

House members who feel the need to speak longer than a minute can make use of another practice known as the Special Order. Special Orders take place after the House has officially ended business for the day. Representatives who have asked in advance are given larger blocks of time to control more or less however they want.

Since the television network C-SPAN now carries all House floor activities live, Special Orders are aimed at the public more than at other members of the House. By the time Special Orders come around, members who are not involved in the Special Orders have usually left the House chamber.

Because they know that many voters are watching, representatives use Special Orders to speak directly to them. As election time nears, some use Special Orders to make what amounts to campaign speeches aimed at their own constituents, but shown live to people all over the country.

Special Orders played a part in swinging Congress—and the nation—to the right, or conservative, side in the 1980s. House Republicans, led by Newt Gingrich of Georgia and Robert Walker of Pennsylvania, used scores of national television hours to attack what they called the "left wing" Democrats. Just as importantly, they used that television time to present almost every public issue in a conservative light.

▶ Nationalizing the House

For almost forty years—from shortly after World War II until 1995—the Democrats held a large majority in the House of Representatives. Because House rules favor the majority party, this meant that the Democrats controlled the House. To many political experts, it seemed almost inevitable that they would go on controlling it for many decades to come.

Although they usually elected Republican

The coming of television has increased the use of visual aids, like the display used here by Senator Byron Dorgan of North Dakota in 1995.

Presidents, they remained stubbornly Democratic, re-electing a majority of Democratic representatives over and over again. Mississippi, for example, voted Republican in presidential elections and even had two Republican senators; yet, all of its representatives were Democrats. One Mississippi Democrat, "Sonny" Montgomery, had served in the House since 1966. Another, Jamie Whitten, had been there since 1941!

The problem for Republicans was how to break the Democrats' hold on the House. It was not enough to find good candidates. Many long-term Democratic representatives had done good service for their constituents. Voters liked them and felt comfortable with them. It was hard for any Republican, no matter how appealing, to break the personal bond that so many voters felt with their Democratic representatives.

The answer that Republican strategists came up with was a joint pledge they called a *Contract With America*, to be signed by Republicans running for the House in 1994. In it they promised that if they were elected they would bring ten specific measures to a vote in the House of Representatives. The measures included tax cuts for middle class families; more defense spending; "get tough" crime measures, such as building more prisons and more use of the death penalty; and welfare, education, and legal reforms.

The *Contract* was, in effect, an attack on the Democratic-run House. It promised that Republicans

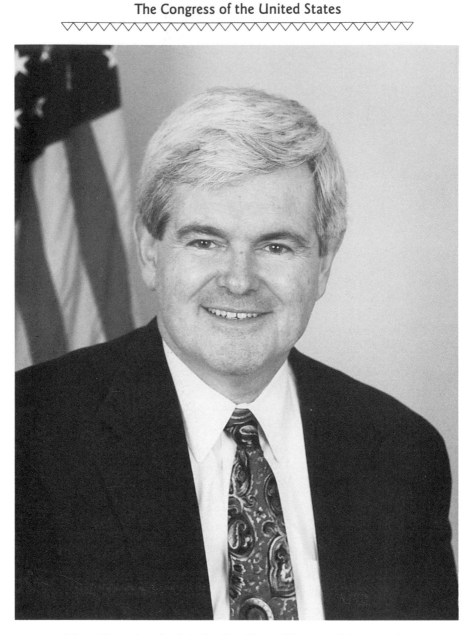

Newt Gingrich, who led the Republican House candidates to their historic victory in the election of 1992, became speaker of the House in the 104th Congress.

would change the way the House did business. They would slash the Congressional budget, trim Congressional staffs, and "[f]orce Congress to live under the same laws as every other American."[1] In the past Congress had excused itself from the labor and civil rights regulations it passed for other people to follow.

The *Contract* also called for limits on how long House members could serve. "Let's replace career politicians with citizen legislators," it said. "After all, politics shouldn't be a lifetime job." [2]

The Republicans' idea was to "nationalize" the House elections. Republicans wanted to change the issue from which candidate the voter preferred to which party—which political philosophy—should control the Congress. And their plan worked. Two hundred and thirty Republicans won seats in the House, giving them a clear majority.

For the first time since 1955, when Joseph W. Martin, Jr., was defeated, a Republican was chosen speaker of the House of Representatives. He was Newt Gingrich of Georgia, the man many people said had invented the strategy of nationalizing the House elections.

Congress quickly passed several provisions of the *Contract*, including one that forced Senate and House members to live under some of the same rules they passed for other Americans. They did not, however, pass the call for term limits.

What Makes Congress Tick?

Congress is a huge and complex institution. In the end, however, what Congress does comes down to people—individual representatives and senators. It comes down to what they want, how they make decisions, and how they vote.

What drives these human beings who make up the Congress of the United States? What makes them tick? Individual representatives and senators are as complex as the institution itself. They act from many different motives and influences. Some of their motives are high and noble, some are low and even cowardly.

Personal and Political Beliefs. Perhaps the most fundamental motives of most members of Congress are their personal beliefs and political ideology. They arrive in Congress complete with their own family history, education, and experiences. That background makes them see the world and political issues in a certain way. Their actions in Congress are bound to reflect that view of the world. Conservative members will tend to vote conservative, liberals to vote liberal.

Party Loyalty and Leadership. Most Republicans tend to vote on one side of bills, and most Democrats on the other. To some extent this reflects their personal beliefs, but it also reflects their party affiliation. Members of the House and Senate will sometimes vote with their party even when they disagree with its position on a particular issue.

One reason for this is party loyalty. They know that if their party is to be effective in combatting the other party within the institution, it needs to act together as much as possible. Another reason is that, when possible, members like to please their party's leadership. Members depend on the leadership in many ways—to put them on a special committee, for example, and to help them in their re-election campaigns.

Sometimes party leadership comes from the White House. Members of the President's party have a natural desire to see the President do well. Even some members of the opposition party believe in supporting the President on certain matters—like those involving defense—whatever their personal views.

Constituents. When members vote opposite to

their party, it is usually in response to the needs or desires of their constituents. Representatives naturally seek to benefit the people they represent. A representative with an auto plant in her district may vote for high tariffs on foreign cars, even though she, and her party, favor free trade in principle.

Critics see this kind of vote as hypocrisy. Representatives respond that they have a duty to represent the interests of their constituents as well as they can.

Personal Ambition. Most politicians are ambitious. They want to achieve and they want to be recognized for their achievements. If they did not, they would not have run for office in the first place. To some degree, then, their actions in Congress are intended to promote their own reputation and to raise their chances of getting re-elected—perhaps even their chance to get elected to a higher office in the future.

Critics of Congress see the drive to get re-elected as a corrupting influence. They say it that it is bad for the country because it leads members to act against their best judgment in order to please the voters. Other observers believe that the desire to get re-elected is healthy for the political system. It helps assure that legislators will represent the voters' wishes, and not just their own opinions.

Public Opinion. Politicians keep a constant eye on public opinion polls. Some hire their own pollsters to keep track of opinion in their own state or district. They do not always blindly follow the swings of that opinion, but they do take it into account. No member wants to get too far away from the beliefs and desires of her or his constituents.

This effort to flow with the tide of public opinion stems from two very different motives. The first may be personal ambition, but the other is a genuine desire to represent the views of their constituents.

Special Interests. One of the most controversial influences on congresspersons are the favors of what is known as the "special interests." A "special interest" group is just that. It is an organization, or segment of society, that has a particular stake in a political issue different from the interests of society as a whole. The defense industry, for example, wants more and more money spent on military weapons, whether or not there is a threat to peace. Unions want higher wages, even if the increase will add to inflation and raise the prices of goods for everyone.

There is nothing evil about special interests as such. We all belong to several special interest groups. We are students or teachers, union members or employers, children or adults or aged, farmers or professionals, and so on.

But organized special interest groups can distort the political process by donating lots of money to the campaigns of politicians who support them. They have a natural desire to help members who agree with them, of course, and a right to support political candidates. But critics charge that special interest money corrupts the politicians who need that money for their campaigns. Some senators and House members, they charge, will vote the way the special interests who contribute to them want them to vote.

Lobbyists. Much of the influence that special interests have on Congress is exerted by lobbyists. These are hired employees of the interest groups who try to meet with members of Congress and make their employers' case.

Some lobbyists are experts in the field—international trade, health care, or whatever—that their employers are interested in. Other lobbyists are experts in the political system. That is, in Congress itself. Many of the most sought after lobbyists are ex-senators and House members, who know the most effective members of Congress personally and know best how to influence them. Whatever their background, the lobbyists' main job is to present their employer's case to the elected representatives.

People who spend 50 percent or more of their working time lobbying Congress are supposed to register with the federal government. Roughly six thousand lobbyists were registered in 1995, although most observers agreed that there were probably many times that number of part-time lobbyists as well.[1]

Taken all together, these tens of thousands of lobbyists have a great deal of influence over the legislative process. Critics claim that their influence is corrupting. Because the groups that they represent contribute lots of money to political campaigns, the critics charge, politicians listen too closely to the lobbyists and are too willing to do their bidding.

Lobbyists respond that they perform a necessary service. The lobbyists often know more about the subjects of bills coming before Congress than the senators and House members do. They help prevent Congress from making mistakes out of ignorance by supplying important information. Concern that the information some lobbyists provide may be misleading is overcome by the fact that there are usually lobbyists on both sides of important issues.

The lobbyists insist that all they really do is act as a voice for the interests—and that means the citizens—they represent. Individual workers, businesspeople, elderly Americans, and others cannot get through to explain their concerns to powerful political leaders. The lobbyists can.

"Lobbying," explained one journalist, is as much a part of democracy, "as any other branch of government."[2] It is certainly an important part of Congress.

The Need to Compromise. In any organization as big as Congress, no individual can get much done by him- or herself. Every member needs the help and support of others. This means cooperation, and cooperation means compromise. Members help each other in the hope that they will be helped in return at some other time. This is, perhaps, the most essential element of all in the way Congress works.

Representing
Diversity

One of the best ways to judge the success of any democratic government is how well it represents minorities. It is easy to represent the majority. After all, elections are decided by the votes of the majority of the people, and bills pass or fail by the votes of a majority of the House and Senate. But what about everyone else?

Tens of millions of Americans vote for losing presidential and Congressional candidates in every election. The majority of people in most states and Congressional districts are white and come from at least two or three generations of families living in the United States. But tens of millions of Americans have another skin color, or are recent immigrants, or are the children or grandchildren of immigrants.

Other Americans are set apart because of physical challenges, or because they belong to an ideological minority.

All of these, along with the other minorities, share many interests with other Americans. They all want a peaceful and prosperous society. They are all concerned with their individual rights, and political freedom to express themselves. But many of these groups also have interests and concerns that arise out of their own special backgrounds.

How are these minorities represented in the Congress of the United States? Any legislature that claims to represent the United States' vastly diverse population has to be rather diverse itself.

Perhaps the least represented of all minorities are those who hold radically different political views. For many years, virtually all members of both houses belonged to one or the other of the two major parties. The only exception has been the independent, Representative Bernie Sanders of Vermont, who is more liberal than the most liberal Democrat.

The House, which is closer to ordinary citizens, has long been the body minorities of all kinds have seen as their best chance to get representation in the federal government. They have, in fact, been elected there in higher proportions than in the Senate.

But minorities are still underrepresented, even in the House, compared to their numbers in the population as a whole. This is particularly true of those minorities who are most recognizable as minorities. Women, for example, make up just over

50 percent of the United States population, but they comprise only about 10 percent of the members in the 104th Congress, and only 8 of the 100 senators.[1]

The nation's most visible ethnic minority groups—African Americans, Hispanic Americans, and Asian Americans—are also underrepresented. Although African Americans make up about 12.5 percent of the United States population,[2] they made up only about 9 percent of the members of the 103rd House.[3] Hispanics make up 9.9 percent of the population, but only 4 percent of House members. Asian Americans and Pacific Islanders make up about 3.5 percent of all Americans, but the four Asian-American congresspersons make up less than 1 percent of the members of the House.[4]

More and more minority representatives *are* being elected, however. Since 1980 the numbers of African-American and Hispanic congresspersons have more than doubled. For the most part these minority representatives have been elected from minority districts. Almost all of the thirty-nine African-American and seventeen Hispanic representatives in the 103rd Congress, for example, represented districts in which a majority of the voters also belonged to the same minorities. There were only two exceptions: Gary Franks of Connecticut, the only Republican African American in the House, and the African-American Democrat Alan Wheat, who came from a mostly white district in Missouri.

Congress in Action—or Congress Inaction?

There is an old joke that says, "The two things people should never watch being made are laws and sausages." In any system where different interests compete to influence the legislative process, law-making is always a messy business. Sometimes, critics charge, it can be an ineffective and even dirty business as well.

No legislation in recent years was more hotly fought over than the health care plan President Bill Clinton sent to the Congress in 1994. Clinton had made the need to reform the nation's health care system a key 1992 campaign issue. Another key issue had been Clinton's—and his Democratic party's—promise to the end gridlock between Congress and the White House.

Although Democrats had controlled Congress for decades, Republicans had controlled the White House for the past twelve years. This made it hard to get things done. Elect a Democratic Congress *and* a Democratic President, the Democrats said, and great things would be accomplished for the nation. The voters took the Democrats at their word and elected Bill Clinton as President, along with a Democratic majority in both the House and the Senate.

▶ The Drive for Health Care Reform

Health care reform was the most important of the great reforms the Democrats hoped to accomplish. They believed that the nation's health care system was bloated and unfair. The United States had excellent doctors, first-class hospitals, and the most advanced medical technology. But the cost of medical care was enormous, and it was going up at a tremendous rate. Even so, people with high incomes or jobs that provided good health insurance plans, got the best health care in the world. People with low and moderate incomes, however, or whose employers did not provide health insurance, got little or no health care except in emergencies.

Something had to be done to lower costs and spread the services more equally, said the President. Polls showed that most people agreed with him. So did many senators and congresspersons in both parties. Almost everyone wanted some kind of reform that would assure good health care for all Americans. It seemed certain that the 103rd Congress, dominated by members of the President's party, would pass an historic overhaul of the health care system.

▶ Controversy

The Democrats in Congress knew that passing a health care bill would not be easy, however. Although everyone wanted reform, everyone seemed to want a different *kind* of reform. Some wanted a comprehensive plan that would guarantee complete health care coverage for everyone, rich or poor, old or young. Others wanted a smaller program that would provide only the most basic coverage for people who could not afford to pay for it themselves.

There was also controversy over *how* health care insurance would be provided and who would pay for it. Some liberals wanted a "single-payer" plan, in which the government would provide health care insurance for everyone. This was the kind of plan that Canada and many European countries had.

Others, including many businesspeople, wanted a more flexible program, in which private insurance companies would continue to provide the insurance plans. The government might help to pay for poor people's insurance, but otherwise it would stay out of health care altogether.

▶ The President's Proposal

President Clinton gave his wife, Hillary Rodham Clinton, the key role in developing a health care reform plan. Together with a top health adviser named Ira Magaziner, she set up a panel of five hundred

First Lady Hillary Rodham Clinton (far right) played a key role in developing the Clinton administration's health care plan.

health care experts, politicians, and others to come up with a workable plan.

The result was a comprehensive plan that would provide health insurance to virtually everyone in the country. It was also incredibly complicated. When printed up and distributed to Congress, the massive proposal took up 1,342 printed pages.[1]

The sheer bulk of the plan turned out to be a political problem. While everybody might like the idea of health care reform in general, there was something in this massive plan for almost everyone to object to.

▶ A Mistake in Timing

President Clinton proposed his health care plan to Congress on September 22, 1993. It seemed like a good time to do it because support for reform was high. But the plan's supporters in Congress were not able to take advantage of the good will and momentum. Congress was about to adjourn, and its members were getting ready to leave Washington for a long recess. Even after they got back, passing the bill would be a long process. Congress might not actually vote on the plan for nearly a year. Any momentum behind the President's program was bound to peter out long before then.

As it turned out the long wait gave plenty of time for opponents of the reform to raise fears about key aspects of the President's program.

▶ The Battle for Public Opinion

The public relations battle over health care reform was bigger and more expensive than any lobbying campaign in history. By midsummer it was estimated that more than $100 million had already been spent by groups on all sides—and that was before the final push to pass a bill had even begun![2]

Ninety-seven different lobbying firms had already been hired to work on health care.[3] Most of them were working to change—or defeat—the Clinton plan. They concentrated most of their efforts on attacking the plan and making people worried about it.

These lobbying firms were successful. Many people became frightened about the plan and what it might mean for them. The key to paying for the new health insurance was a government mandate, or command, that large employers pay 80 percent of the cost for their full-time employees. This upset many employers, who claimed that they could not afford to pay so much.

Employers were not the only ones who were worried. People who worked for small employers or who only worked part-time worried that they might have to pay too much out of their own pockets. People who already had good health insurance worried that the new plan would cost more than what they were paying now and might not provide as much coverage.

▶ The Lobbyists

Lobbyists working against the plan were already waiting when the legislators returned to Washington in early 1994. A lot was at stake, and the lobbyists would continue to jam the halls of Congress until the issue was decided.

Many representatives were more than willing to listen to them. After all, some of the plan's most powerful opponents—including the medical insurance industry and the American Medical Association—were among the biggest contributors to election campaigns. At least $25 million of that first $100 million dollars was spent in the form of campaign contributions.[4]

No politicians would ever publicly admit that they changed their votes on health care because a big campaign contributor told them to, but Congressional enthusiasm for the reforms faded fast while campaign contributions by opponents of the plan rose. "This is what messes up everything in Washington," complained Senator Russ Feingold of Wisconsin, a supporter of reform, "the unholy connection between campaign [funding] and legislation."[5]

Not all the lobbying money was spent on influencing Congress directly, however. A big chunk of it was spent to change the public's mind about health care reform. Lobbyists know that one of the best ways to influence Congress is to influence voters.

The insurance industry launched a major television ad campaign featuring a fictional middle-class married couple named Harry and Louise. Harry and Louise seemed sympathetic to health care reform at first. But then, in ad after ad, they were seen reading details of the plan to each other, and being alarmed at what they saw. The intention of the commercials, of course, was to alarm television viewers as well.

The insurance companies were not the only ones to appeal to television viewers. The drug companies had a separate campaign to convince the public to support them if reform threatened their industry.

The nation's largest labor union organization, the AFL-CIO, had its own television ad campaign that supported the President's plan. The AFL-CIO and other supporters were heavily outspent by the enemies of the proposed reforms, however. The Harry and Louise campaign alone cost more than three times what the unions put into the pro-reform ads.[6]

Some opponents attacked the plan in principle. They insisted that government should stay out of health care altogether. But other opponents actually supported parts of the plan, even while attacking others. Drug companies, for example, liked the proposal to have the government pay for prescription drugs, but they opposed those parts designed to hold down drug prices. Roman Catholic bishops liked the idea of universal health care, but they bitterly attacked a provision that made abortion available under the plan.

Few of the special interest groups, except the unions, put much effort into supporting the parts of the plan they liked. Instead they concentrated on attacking what they did not like about it. The overwhelming effect was negative. Piece by piece, support for the plan was being whittled down, even before Congressional committees began to vote on any proposed bills.

▶ In the Committees

One way or another any health care reform bill would affect almost every area of national life. This meant that many committees of Congress had a duty to study the bill and report their findings. Several of those committees took a hand at rewriting all or part of the bill.

Before long there was not one health care reform bill, but several. No less than five committees came out with new bills of their own. Six other committees came out with major changes they hoped to make to whichever bill was passed.[7]

With this kind of competition, it was clear that the President's plan was bound to fail. Most observers still believed that *some* major health care reform would come out of the 103rd Congress, but it would not be the one President Clinton had asked for. Congress would write its own health care reform bill. But how would Congress go about it, and what kind of bill would it be?

▶ Partisan Politics

Congress itself was badly split over health care reform, and along many lines. By far the deepest split, however, was the partisan one. Most Republicans opposed the President's plan from the start. Some opposed it because they thought it was poorly designed or because they did not like the idea of the government expanding its role in health care. But others opposed it because it was the *President's* plan and they opposed the President. No Republicans wanted to see a Democratic President score a big legislative success in an election year.

Many Republicans were convinced that denying him that success would be good politics. It was also tit for tat. As Senator John McCain of Arizona pointed out, many Republicans were bitter. In the previous election year, when the Republican George Bush was President, the Democrats had "basically blocked the entire Bush agenda." Now the Republicans were "doing no less" to Clinton.[8]

▶ Split Among the Democrats

Republican opposition would not matter, however, if the Democrats held together. This fact may have led the Democratic leaders in Congress to make a big mistake. Instead of trying to split the moderate Republicans, looking for some who might be willing to help write a new Congressional health care bill to substitute for the President's plan, the Democrats apparently decided to pass the bill on their own.

But the Democrats in Congress were split among themselves. Even those who enthusiastically supported health care reform were not willing to accept the plan as the President presented it. Some powerful Democrats had strong objections to particular parts of the bill. Others had ideas of their own about what kinds of benefits ought to be provided or what kinds of taxes should be used to pay for them. Still others saw a chance to get into the history books. This was major legislation, and they wanted to make their marks on it.

In House and Senate offices all over the Capitol, Democrats and Republicans were meeting to plan their own versions of health care reform. But for the most part, they were not meeting together. Many were not even trying to come up with a bill that would pass. "Progressive" Democrats met to find ways to promote a single-payer plan, even though they knew that the majority would never support that kind of plan. "Conservative" Republicans met to block any expansion of the federal government's role in health care. Only a handful of "moderates" made a serious effort to work out a compromise that might be acceptable to a majority of both houses.

Senator John Danforth of Missouri, who was considered one of the most moderate Republicans, led a group that claimed to be willing to compromise with the Democrats to pass some kind of health care

Not all senators and representatives have offices in the Capitol. Many, for example, work here, in the Reborn Office Building.

bill. But "massive surgery would be required," said Danforth, before they could support even the most moderate Democrat proposals.[9]

Meanwhile other Republicans were making it clear that they opposed *any* government health care plan. Some sounded as if they were opposed to any government plan to do anything at all. "If the 20th century proves anything," declared Senator Phil Gramm of Texas, "it is that government does not work."[10]

The opponents did everything they could to slow down the process. The Democrats, they complained, were just trying to rush a bill—any bill—through Congress before the elections. Supporters responded that health care reform had waited far too long already. "President Truman proposed [national health care reform] in the 1940s," exclaimed House Majority Leader Richard Gephardt. "President Nixon proposed it in the 1970s; I don't think to act on it in 50 years is rushing anything."[11]

▶ Mitchell and Gephardt

With so many plans flying around Congress, could any one of them survive? Clearly any bill that would pass the heavily Democratic Congress would have to have strong Democratic support. Therefore, attention soon focused on two different bills sponsored by Democratic leaders in Congress.

In the House, Majority Leader Richard Gephardt proposed a relatively liberal plan. It was based on the President's original plan, as altered by no less than eight different House committees. Like the

President's proposal, the Gephardt plan promised universal health care coverage by the year 1999.

In the Senate, Majority Leader George Mitchell of Maine offered a more moderate bill that he said would provide coverage for 95 percent of all Americans by the year 2000.

Although health care reform was in the hands of Congress now, many Democrats still looked to the President for leadership. Would he support Mitchell's or Gephardt's bill? Or would he hold out for something more like his own plan?

Although the President really wanted a much stronger and more comprehensive measure, he announced support for *both* the Mitchell bill in the Senate *and* the Gephardt bill in the House. He seemed to be willing to compromise in order to get almost *any* bill that might lead to universal health care some time in the future. The progressives, who wanted a more ambitious plan, charged that the President was not compromising—he was surrendering.

▶ Floor Action Begins—And Stops

What was expected to be a historic floor debate on the Mitchell bill began in the Senate on August 9, 1994. Two senators, Gramm of Texas and Shelby of Alabama, threatened to filibuster against it. Were they trying to force the Democrats to compromise ever further? No, declared Shelby. They were not interested in improving the bill. "We want to kill it."[12]

Only a few hours later, however, Shelby backed down. If really major changes were made, he

As House majority leader in 1993, Representative Richard Gephardt of Missouri sponsored an alternative health care bill to that of his Democratic President.

suggested, something might be worked out.[13] Prospects for passing some kind of reform seemed to be looking up.

The next day the Senate Democrats managed to defeat a Republican measure to delay any action at all on health care for a year. The Republicans had tried to delay because they expected to make some gains in the upcoming elections, and so hoped to have more power to shape—or defeat—a health care bill in the next Congress.

Meanwhile the Republican Senate Minority Leader Bob Dole announced a new Republican health care bill. Dole's proposal, which was much smaller than the Democrats' measures, was bound to fail, but Republicans hoped it would give some of the Democrats who were unhappy with the Mitchell bill a Republican alternative to vote for.

In fact, there would be many alternatives. A number of plans were going to be offered, some liberal and some conservative. The vote would probably be "king of the hill." That is, the plans would be voted on one at a time, in a particular order determined by the leadership. Each member could vote "yes" or "no" on each plan. Any one or all of the plans might pass. The last one to pass would be "king of the hill"—the one which would be sent to the President to be signed into law.

This meant that everybody had a plan that they could vote for, safe in the knowledge that it would not pass. This was good for politicians hoping for re-election in states and districts where health care

Senator Bob Dole of Kansas, who sponsored the main Republican health care bill in 1993, became Senate majority leader the next year.

reform was highly controversial. They could tell voters that they had voted for health care reform, without taking the blame for elements of actual reform that large groups of voters did not like.

However slowly, events seemed to be moving toward the historic vote on health care in the Senate. Then, all of a sudden, action on health care was brought to a crashing halt. It had been blindsided by a totally unexpected vote on an entirely different bill in the House of Representatives.

▶ Crime or Health Care?

The President's second most important proposal before Congress was a massive anticrime bill. It would supply federal money for as many as a hundred thousand new police, build new prisons, and pay for a number of new social programs to help young people in rough neighborhoods overcome the temptation of crime. It would also ban the especially deadly military-style guns known as assault weapons.

The President's crime bill had sailed through both houses of Congress once already. But, because the House and Senate versions of the bill had the usual differences, they had gone to a conference committee. Many changes had been made in conference. The new crime bill that resulted was bigger and more ambitious than either version that had passed earlier. It was also billions of dollars more expensive.

The conference bill would pass the House as easily as the earlier bill had done, but if even a single amendment was added in the Senate, it would mean that the bill had to go back to the House to be considered all over again. The crime bill could be delayed indefinitely—and that would mean that the health care bill would probably be delayed as well.

Crime came first. The whole legislative program of the Democrats and their President was in danger of crashing down around them. All the attention of both Houses suddenly refocused on the crime bill.

It was a short but bitter battle, with the powerful lobbying arm of the National Rifle Association (NRA) fighting hard to defeat the gun control measures in the bill. "This is about guns, guns, guns, guns," Senator Biden of Delaware declared.[14] The NRA was important because it had lots of members who voted in Congressional elections and because it gave large amounts of money to political campaigns. Many members of both parties were friendly to the NRA, and many more were afraid of them.

Other factors worked against the crime bill as well. With the election coming closer, some Republicans hoped to give the President another crushing defeat. Even so there were Republicans who supported the bill. Some were afraid to vote against a crime bill in an election year. Others were determined to fight crime even if it helped a Democratic President. In the end the President and the bill's supporters in Congress won. The crime bill passed.

▶ The Death of Health Care Reform

The Democrats won the crime bill battle, but only by losing the health care war. Moderate Republicans who had supported the crime bill were not about to hand the President another victory. Among them was John Danforth, who had once held out the hope of a compromise on health care reform. Meanwhile Democrats who had angered the NRA by voting for the crime bill were not about to bring the anger of the health insurance industry down on them as well.

The very day after the crime bill was sent to the President to sign, Senator Mitchell announced that he was dropping the effort to pass health care reform in the Senate. He would not be able to pass a major health bill in the current Congress, he declared. It was no use trying.

Does Congress Work?

When President Clinton presented the 103rd Congress with his plan in 1993, health care reform was something that everybody wanted. Public opinion polls showed that Americans heavily favored overhauling the health care insurance system, and those polls were backed up by the 1992 election returns. The voters elected both a President who promised reform and many new members of Congress who had also campaigned on the issue. A clear majority of both houses seemed committed to reform the health care system. And yet health care reform was defeated by that same Congress.

As we have seen a variety of factors contributed to that defeat: partisan politics; bad timing by the President and his supporters; the fear of senators and representatives to cast controversial votes in an election year; lobbyists; a massive public relations campaign; the failure of liberals and moderates, and Republicans and Democrats, to compromise; the complicated procedures of the House and Senate committee systems; and the battle over the crime bill. All of these factors and more combined to kill health care reform.

The way people felt about the defeat of health care reform depended, to a great extent, on how they had felt about the reforms. Supporters of reform were angry, while opponents were pleased.

But for some political observers the defeat of such a popular measure raised bigger questions.

- Does Congress really work? Does it actually represent the people of the United States? Or is the system so clumsy or so corrupt—that it can no longer do the necessary work of government?
- Do the rules of Congress make gridlock and inaction inevitable?
- Is it too easy for special interest groups to overcome the will of most Americans?

These are serious questions, and some people think that the answer to them is "yes." They believe that Congress needs more reform than the nation's health care system ever did.

Suggestions for reform include changing the way representatives and senators are elected, and the lengths of their terms. Many people favor a Constitutional amendment to limit the number of terms

In 1993, President Bill Clinton won one big fight in Congress—the crime bill—but lost an even bigger one—health care reform.

they can serve as well. In order to cut down the power of the special interests, some reformers call for limiting the amount of money candidates can spend on election campaigns—or even paying for campaigns entirely by tax money instead of by private contributions.

Reforms like these may or may not be good ideas. But the need for them is hardly proven by the defeat of the health care reform measures in 1994. In fact, defenders of Congress might take heart from the action—and the inaction—of the 103rd Congress.

The fact that Congress could not act on health care reform does not mean that it could not act on anything. The same session that failed to pass the controversial health care measure did pass a controversial crime bill.

What's more, Congress may actually have been doing the will of the people when it defeated the health care measures. Although health care reform was a popular idea in 1993, it was not nearly as popular in 1994. By the time the reform effort died in Congress, at least one poll showed that more than 50 percent of Americans hoped that Congress would not act on health care reform in that session. "[P]eople have become so afraid of what health care reform might do to them that they're relieved nothing is getting through this year," said Senator Richard Lugar of Indiana.[1]

In the long run, even supporters of health care reform might feel that the 103rd Congress did them a favor. After all, health care reform did not die in the 103rd Congress, only a handful of specific health care reform proposals died there. In reality, no one was very happy with any of the measures that had been introduced. Liberals thought they were too timid. Conservatives thought they were too radical. Moderates had doubts in both directions.

The 104th Congress, which was elected later that same year, was expected to take up health care reform again. If it did, it might produce a better bill than the proposals before the 103rd Congress. And even if the 104th Congress failed to act, the 105th Congress might take up the issue. Or perhaps the 106th Congress, which will be elected in the year 2000.

If no future Congress passes health care reform, it will be because the nation decides that health care reform is not needed after all. Congress is a democratic body. In the long run, it tends to follow the will of the people of the United States as expressed in national elections. That is true, whether that will is right or wrong, wise or foolish. Congress will never be much better, or much worse, than the voters who choose its members. When we, the American people, become dissatisfied with the action—or the inaction—of Congress, perhaps we need to examine ourselves,

Finally what is most important about the Congress of the United States is not what any particular session of Congress does or does not do. Congress is an ongoing institution. It has survived for more than two centuries, and it may go on for much longer than that in the future.

Congress is certainly not perfect and it often makes mistakes. But the mistakes of one session of Congress can be corrected by another one. Over the course of history the Congress of the United States has served the country as well as any legislature in the world.

Glossary

amendment—A change made in a bill or law; as in, an amendment to a bill or a Constitutional amendment. Congress has the power to enact Constitutional amendments, which then have to be ratified by three-fourths of the states before they become law.

bill—A proposed law, considered by a legislature.

civil, as in "civil law"—*Civil* is sometimes used as opposed to *criminal* when referring to laws. It distinguishes laws involving wrongs committed against individuals. Violations of civil laws are usually settled by lawsuits brought by individuals who have been wronged, rather than by the government.

Congress—The United States Congress, the legislature of the national government, which consists of both the Senate and the House of Representatives.

Congressional—Having to do with Congress.

conservative—One who favors the status quo, or in current politics, one who supports the social and economic views of the modern Republican party.

constituent—A person represented by someone else. *Constituents* can refer specifically to the voters of an area or to everyone who lives there.

criminal, as in "criminal law"—*Criminal* is sometimes used as opposed to *civil* when referring to laws. It distinguishes laws against crimes. That is, acts which are considered offenses against all of society—including acts of violence against individuals—and which are prosecuted by some level of government (federal, state, or local).

Democrat—A member of the Democratic party.

Glossary

Democratic—In American politics, having to do with the Democratic party.

democracy—A government either run by or elected by the citizens.

federal—In the United States, having to do with national—as opposed to state—matters.

house—When written with a lower case *h, house* can be used for either body of Congress; as in, "the Senate is the smaller of the two houses." When written with a capital *h*, it is used to refer to the House of Representatives.

legislator—One who makes laws.

legislature—A body that makes laws for a state or a nation.

override—To pass over a veto. A two-thirds vote by both houses of Congress can override a presidential veto.

partisan—Having to do with, or depending on, particular political parties.

pass—To approve a bill and send it on to the next step in the legislative process.

popular vote—The votes cast by ordinary citizens. Members of Congress are directly elected by popular vote. The President, however, is chosen indirectly by the electoral college.

pork—Unnecessary provisions, requiring the spending of federal money, added to a bill in order to benefit particular representatives or their constituents.

ratify—To approve. Amendments to the Constitution have to be ratified by three-fourths of the states.

recognize—To take notice of someone. When a member of Congress is recognized, he or she is free to speak on the floor.

represent—To act in the place of or on behalf of others.

∇∇∇∇∇∇∇∇∇∇∇∇∇∇∇∇∇∇∇∇∇∇∇∇∇∇∇∇∇∇∇∇∇∇∇∇

republic—A country in which government officials are elected, and the ultimate power rests with the people.

Republican—In American politics, having to do with the Republican party.

Senate of the United States—The smallest of the two federal legislative bodies.

United States House of Representatives—The largest of the two federal legislative bodies.

veto—A presidential power. The President can prevent a law passed by Congress from becoming a law by vetoing, or disapproving, it. Congress can, however, put the bill into effect over the President's veto by repassing it with a two-thirds majority in each house.

whip—A partisan Congressional or Senatorial official whose job is to help plan and organize his or her party's activities.

Chapter Notes

Chapter 1

1. *Constitution of the United States*, Article II, Section 4.

Chapter 2

1. *Declaration of Independence*, 1776.

2. Quoted, Paul M. Angle, *By These Words* (New York: Rand McNally and Company, 1954), p. 46.

3. Fred R. Harris, *America's Democracy: The Ideal and the Reality* (Glenview, Ill.: Scott, Foresman and Company, 1980), p. 34.

Chapter 3

1. *Constitution of the United States*, Article III, Section 2.

2. Ibid.

3. Ibid., Article I, Section 1.

4. Ibid., Section 2.

5. Ibid., Section 3.

6. Ibid., Section 8.

7. Ibid., Article III, Section 3.

8. Ibid., Article IV, Section 3.

9. Ibid.

10. Ibid., Article I, Sections 2 and 3.

11. Ibid., Article V.

12. Ibid., Amendment XII

13. Ibid., Article II, Section 2.

14. For more discussion of this issue, see Michael Kronenwetter's *The Military Power of the President* (New York: Franklin Watts, 1988).

15. *Constitution of the United States*, Article I, Section VIII.

16. United States Supreme Court decision in the case of *McCulloch* v. *Maryland*, 4 Wheat. 17 United States 316 (1819).

17. *Constitution of the United States*, Article I, Section VII.

18. Fred R. Harris, *America's Democracy: The Ideal and the Reality* (Glenview, Ill.: Scott, Foresman and Company, 1980), p. 557.

19. *Constitution of the United States*, Amendment I.

20. Ibid., Amendment X.

21. Ibid., Amendment XIII, Section II.

Chapter 4

1. *Constitution of the United States*, Article I, Sections 2 and 3.

Chapter 5

1. *Constitution of the United States*, Article I, Section 3.

2. 1993 populations, Bureau of the Census figures, United States Department of Commerce.

3. Speaking on *Saturday Journal*, C-SPAN cable television network, May 13, 1995.

4. *Evans and Novak*, CNN television network, October 8, 1994.

5. William H. Young, *Ogg and Ray's Introduction to American Government*, 12th ed. (New York: Appleton-Century-Crofts, 1962), p. 306.

6. *Chronicle of the Twentieth Century* (Mount Kisco, N.Y.: Chronicle Publications, 1987), p. 732.

7. Senator George Mitchell, Senate majority leader in the 103rd Congress, speaking on C-SPAN, October 7, 1994.

Chapter 6

1. *Contract with America*.

2. Ibid.

Chapter 7

1. Discussion at "Media Perspective on Lobbying Issues," conducted by the Lobbying Institute, at American University, Washington, D.C., cablecast live on C-SPAN, June 4, 1993.

2. Jeff Birnbaum of the *Wall Street Journal*, speaking at "Media Perspective."

Chapter 8

1. 1990 United States Census.

2. *The World Almanac and Book of Facts 1995* (Mahwah, N.J.: World Almanac, 1994), p. 373.

3. The latest Congress for which figures are available.

4. Bob Minzesheimer, "Most House Minorities' Seats Safe," *USA Today*, October 24, 1994.

Chapter 9

1. Jill Smolowe, "A Bloody Clash of Egos," *Time*, April 4, 1994, p. 28.

2. Ceci Connolly, "Storming the Capital," *Congressional Quarterly Weekly Report*, July 23, 1994, p. 2042.

3. Ibid.

4. Ibid.

5. Karen J. Cohen, "Feingold's Hopes on Health Dashed," *Milwaukee Sentinel*, August 24, 1994.

6. Margaret Carlson, "Harry and Louise," *Time*, March 7, 1994.

7. "Social Policy: Issue, Health Care Overhaul," *Congressional Quarterly Weekly Report*, November 5, 1994.

8. "Hard Fought Crime Bill Battle Spoils Field for Health Care," *Congressional Quarterly Weekly Report*, August 27, 1994.

9. C-SPAN, August 10, 1994.

10. Senator Phil Gramm of Texas, speaking in the Senate health care debate, August 11, 1994.

11. "With Outcome Still Uncertain, Members Face Critical Vote." *Congressional Quarterly*, August 6, 1994.

12. National Public Radio news report, August 9, 1994.

13. CNN news reports, August 9, 1994.

14. Senate debate on the crime bill, Aug. 24, 1994.

Chapter 10

1. Dan Goodgame, "The High Price of Gridlock," *Time*, October 10, 1994, pp. 31–32.

Further Reading

Congressional Quarterly's Guide to Congress. 3rd Edition. Washington, D.C.: Congressional Quarterly, 1982.

Fenno, Richard F. *Congressmen in Committees*. Boston: Little, Brown, 1973.

Greider, William. *Who Will Tell the People?* New York: Touchstone, 1993.

Harris, Fred R. *America's Democracy: The Ideal and the Reality*. Glenview, Ill.: Scott, Foresman and Company, 1980.

Joseph, Alvin M., Jr. *The American Heritage History of the Congress of the United States*. New York: American Heritage, 1975.

Kronenwetter, Michael. *How Democratic Is the United States?* New York: Watts, 1994.

MacNeil, Neil. *Forge of Democracy*. New York: David McKay, 1963.

Peters, Charles. *How Washington Really Works*. Reading, Mass.: Addison-Wesley, 1980.

Wolpe, Bruce C. *Lobbying Congress: How the System Works*. Washington, D.C.: Congressional Quarterly, 1990.

Young, William H. *Ogg and Ray's Introduction to American Government*. 12th Edition. New York: Appleton-Century-Crofts, 1962.

Index